Chronic Adventure: The Ultimate RPG Campaign Creator Guidebook

AMY N. KAPLAN

Cover Illustration by Ivan Nikulin

An imprint of Misfit Pages

Misfit Games
Published by Misfit Pages
Texas USA

On the World Wide Web at www.misfitpages.com
First Published 2024

Cover Art
Ivan Nikulin

ISBN: 978-1-962613-06-4 (First Edition)
ISBN: 978-1-962613-05-7 (Digital Edition)
ISBN: 978-1-962613-21-7 (Audio Edition)

Preface

As an avid tabletop RPG player for over three decades, I've had the pleasure of adventuring through fantastical worlds brought to life by talented Game Masters. Their lovingly crafted settings, populations of lively NPCs, and epic story arcs kept our parties engaged week after week. After participating in so many memorable campaigns, I was inspired to try my hand at game mastering.

Over the years, I've run games in homebrew worlds, published settings, and everything in between. Through trial and error, I've learned techniques for building immersive worlds, planning compelling adventures, and guiding players through unforgettable journeys. The lessons I've picked up fill the pages of this campaign creation guidebook.

My goal with this book is to provide fellow Game Masters, both experienced and aspiring, with tools, templates, and tips for crafting their own RPG campaigns. I aim to help GMs bring their unique creative visions to the table. While each group's play style differs, the foundations of prep work remain essential. My hope is that the framework and advice presented here will empower GMs to build campaigns tailor-made for their players.

Join me on a journey through the realms of worldbuilding, storycrafting, and adventure planning. Let's equip our toolboxes with templates and guides that turn our wildest imaginative dreams into thrilling RPG campaigns. The quest to become a great Game Master starts here!

Table of Contents

Let's Begin!

So, you're ready to be a Game Master (aka GM or DM). You've played the game, you've bought the books, and now you want to run the game. Fantastic! This campaign builder supplement will help guide you through the process of creating your own homebrew campaign. If this isn't your first homebrew campaign, you can skip ahead. For the rest of you, read on and we'll break down what each page is for. Keep in mind that all campaigns don't need to use all the pages I mention here.

What do we need to begin? Make sure you have your copy of **Chronicles of Adventure: The Ultimate RPG Campaign Builder** and some pencils. If you didn't buy the book, that's okay! You'll need a binder, binder tabs (or dividers), some looseleaf paper, grid paper (or whatever your preference for map making is), some pencils and maybe even some pens or colored pencils.

Before we get into actually writing your campaign, we'll need to do a little groundwork. You'll need to create 18 sections for your binder. I'll list them out for you.

- Brainstorming
- Campaign Summary
- Player Characters
- The World
- Local Settings
- Player Character Creation Notes
- Back Stories
- Mysteries
- Scenarios
- Random Events and Encounters
- Traps and Puzzles

- Loot
- Adversary List
- Adversaries
- NPC List
- NPCs
- Maps
- Notes

Now you're ready to build your campaign. I've included images and drawings from the printed version of **Chronicles of Adventure: The Ultimate RPG Campaign Builde**r for you in the appendix as well as a few examples of handouts and guides I've used.

We'll be jumping around a bit at first, but after your first campaign you'll be able to fill this in without help. Let's get started on your campaign!

Brainstorming

The Brainstorming section is perhaps the most important part of creating your own campaign. This is where you let your imagination run wild and come up with the core ideas that will drive your entire story. Don't worry about getting it "right" at this stage - just write down any ideas that come to you. The goal here is to get those creative juices flowing!

To start, think about the overall theme or premise of your campaign. What will this adventure ultimately be about? Is it a sprawling epic fantasy? A tense political thriller? A lighthearted romp? The premise shapes everything else, so spend some time on this. You could start with a basic concept like "unlikely heroes band together to save the world" or "a heist gone wrong uncovers greater evils."

Next, consider the problem or goal the party is trying to accomplish. This gives the story direction and drive. Maybe they need to overthrow an evil tyrant, solve an ancient mystery, or reunite two star-crossed lovers. Defining the party's central objective gets you thinking about plot and conflict.

With your premise and goal in mind, think about where this adventure takes place - the setting or location. The possibilities are endless - a vast desert kingdom, an enchanted forest, a bustling trade city, the Nine Hells. The geography shapes the tone and feel of the world. Also consider the time period. Is it medieval fantasy? Steampunk future? The when and where provide context.

Now onto characters. Start brainstorming key NPCs, particularly antagonists with evil plans. A great villain drives the action forward and challenges the party. Maybe an evil wizard wants to unlock an ancient evil, or a dragon covets a stolen treasure hoard. Fleshing out the villain's motivations and machinations generates plot hooks and conflicts.

Speaking of plot hooks, jot down any side quest or adventure ideas that come to mind, even if they don't fit neatly into the main story yet. Unexpected diversions keep things interesting. Maybe the party finds a treasure map, stumbles upon a village under attack, or gets caught up in local village drama. You can weave these in later.

Consider throwing in a midpoint surprise or plot twist to shake things up. These revelations change the nature of the quest and raise the stakes. Perhaps the party's patron is not who they seem. Or the villain is secretly the king's lost son. Twists introduce complexity and moral shades of grey.

Brainstorm an epic climax where the party faces their biggest challenge. This is the final showdown where everything is on the line. It could be confronting the big bad villain once and for all, solving an impossible puzzle, or storming an enemy stronghold. Go big and get creative!

If you have a secondary quest or goal in mind, sketch it out too. This provides layers beyond the main story arc. Maybe they need to collect three magical artifacts while pursuing the villain. Or the party gets caught up in a local dispute. Subplots add dimension.

Think about clues or secrets the party needs to uncover along the way. These propel the mystery forward. Ancient prophecies, hidden treasure maps, obscure runes - make the party work to piece together the full picture. Information revealed bit by bit keeps things captivating.

Finally, make a to-do list of any other ideas you want to expand on later - locations, NPCs, magic items, puzzles. This campaign brainstorming page is for generating ideas. Refine and organize them into a cohesive story during the next steps.

Let your imagination go wild during this brainstorming process! The key is to get your raw creative ideas flowing without overthinking anything. You can tweak and polish things later. Every campaign starts as a spark of inspiration, so let yours take shape on the page. The possibilities are endless - pick the threads that excite you and start weaving your unique tale. This is your world - build it!

The World

Now let's skip ahead to **The World** pages. This section is your chance to sketch out the basics of the world your players will adventure in. While detailed worldbuilding can be fun, resist the urge to meticulously detail every aspect of your world before starting. Focus on establishing just enough to give your players context and inspiration.

Start by thinking about the core elements:

- Time Period: What is the general technological/social level? Medieval? Ancient? Futuristic?
- Geography: What are the major physical regions and landmarks? Sketch out a simple map.
- Factions: Who holds power? sketch out the basic political/social landscape.
- Religion: What, if any, are the major belief systems? How do they influence society?
- Magic: How common/rare is magic? What are its origins and limitations?
- History: What are 1-3 key events that shaped this world? Jot down a timeline.

Aim for giving each element 2-3 sentences or bullet points of summary. Provide just enough for players to latch onto and ask questions. Treat this as a starting point to build from, not a final product.

As your campaign progresses, collaborate with your players to add more detail to whatever interests them. Maybe they want more info on a specific religion or city - then you can expand on that area before the next session. Let your world grow organically from play, rather than trying to complete it beforehand.

Most importantly, make sure your players have context to make meaningful choices and take actions in your world. If you've given them that foundation, you're off to a great start! The rest will come through playing together.

You can include a calendar, if necessary, to show what the passage of time will be like in your world. There's ample space for this, but you really don't need much more than 2 pages to get started. While you're working on this you may need to sketch out a few **Maps.** Use whatever map format works best for you here, hex, grid or dot. You don't need all the details in the beginning. You can fill it in as you need to.

What Do My Players Need to Know for Character Creation

From **The World** we want to go to **What Do My Players Need to Know for Character Creation.** Character creation is one of the most important parts of starting a new campaign. As the Game Master, you'll need to provide your players with clear guidelines and limitations for creating their characters. This will ensure everyone is on the same page and help avoid confusion down the line. When outlining the character creation process, be sure to cover the following:

System Rules

The first thing to establish is what system and sourcebooks you'll be using. Specify which core rulebooks are allowed, as well as any supplemental materials. Make it clear upfront if you'll be using any house rules or tweaks to the standard rules.

Races

Detail what fantasy races are available for play in your setting. Classic options include humans, elves, dwarves, halflings, and half-orcs. But you can get more creative, introducing uncommon races like dragonborn, tieflings, aarakocra, and more. Provide a brief description of each playable race and any innate abilities or attributes they possess. Specify if there are any restrictions, such as limiting certain races to particular classes or regions within your world.

Classes

Outline what classes and subclasses are open to players. Some options include fighters, wizards, clerics, rogues, and more. But many other classes exist across supplements, so specify exactly which ones can be chosen. You might restrict access to certain classes to better fit your setting. Also note any changes you're implementing, such as tweaks to class features or restrictions on certain subclasses.

Backgrounds

Most systems include backgrounds which further define a character's origins and upbringing. Provide a list of available backgrounds or give players tools to customize their own. Make sure to mention if you're banning any background options that don't fit your setting or campaign.

Languages

Determine what languages exist in your world and provide rules for what languages each race can speak by default. You'll also need to outline how players can learn additional languages through class features, backgrounds, or spending skill points. Make sure to include both standard languages like Elvish and Dwarvish as well as any unique languages you've created for your setting.

Ability Score Generation

Clarify how you want ability scores (Strength, Dexterity, etc) to be generated. The standard options include point-buy, standard array, and different dice rolling methods. Outline the method you prefer or allow players to choose from 2-3 balanced options. Make sure your rules for generating scores align with any racial ability score modifiers.

Alignment

Establish if alignment restrictions will be used and what the available alignment options are. In most campaigns, all nine alignments are open to players. But in some cases, certain alignments may be banned if they don't fit your setting or story. At minimum, specify whether players can choose any alignment or if you're restricting options.

Gods & Religion

Optional rules exist for integrating gods into character backgrounds and clerical powers. Decide how involved religion will be in your campaign and what deities exist in your world for players to follow. If you're using them, provide a brief overview of each god and their domains, alignment, symbols, and clerical abilities. Also clarify if you're allowing non-standard clerics who don't follow a specific deity.

Starting Level

Indicate what level you want players to begin at. The standard is Level 1, but some DMs prefer higher starting levels between 3-5. This allows players to begin with more abilities and hit points. Just keep in mind encounters will need to be balanced for the starting level.

House Rules

Lastly, outline any important house rules, adjustments or limitations you're implementing that weren't already covered. This might include things like:

- No evil-aligned characters
- Restrictions on certain feats or abilities
- Maximum number of a specific race/class combination
- Specific ability score requirements for certain classes
- Custom skills, backgrounds, or languages

Provide sufficient detail on character creation to avoid confusion, but leave some areas open for creative input from your players. Encourage them to ask questions and work with them to ensure their concepts fit the campaign. Character creation sets the tone for the whole game, so starting it off right is crucial. With clear guidelines and limitations, you'll be on track for a great campaign!

I had a special handout for my players when I ran RPGs. Here are a few "highlights" to give you some ideas:

- How much can you carry?
    - You have space for 24 unique items in your backpack
    - You can carry an additional 4 bags
    - You can only put empty bags into other bags

- Extra Gear
  - You can only wear two rings on each hand
  - You can only wear one necklace
  - You can only wear one item on your wrist at a time
- Magical Items
  - Magical Items have 5 uses of their magical ability
  - You must always roll to hit to use the ability
  - A failed roll counts as a use
- Professions or Proficiencies
  - You can visit a town to learn new professions
    - Learning a new profession will cost money
    - You must buy any gear associated with that profession
  - You must be carrying your "tools of the trade" with you in order to use your profession.
  - Crafting any single item using your profession will take a long rest, as long as you have all of the ingredients necessary.
  - Exceptions to the time it takes to craft:
    - Painter can sketch a quick map... there will not be a lot of detail
    - Cartographer can create a quick map that does not have a lot of detail... it will not be to scale and will only show rough outlines of roads and terrain
    - A weaver can quickly throw a few stitches into something to mend a hole

Local Settings

The Local Settings section is where you will establish the foundation for your entire campaign. This is your opportunity to vividly portray the world your players will be immersed in. Take your time with this section and don't skimp on the details - a rich, vibrant setting is key to player engagement and immersion.

When describing your world, start big picture. Give a broad overview of the prominent nations, continents, or regions. Who is in charge in these areas? What are the systems of government like? Are there empires, monarchies, democracies? Provide just enough detail to give your players a sense of the power structures at play.

Next, zoom in on the specific area or city where the campaign will take place. Describe the local landscapes, architecture, weather, and culture. Really help your players visualize what it would be like for their characters to live here.

Sketch out the major local factions, who runs them, and their goals. These could be competing merchant houses, gangs, religious sects, schools of magic, or secret societies. Detail any tensions or alliances between factions that could impact the campaign.

Give your players a sense of what daily life is like by describing common resources like shops, inns, temples, taverns, etc. Come up with names and proprietors for frequently visited places so they feel rooted in the world.

Be sure to create memorable NPCs to populate the world. Give each one a name, personality, background, and motivations. Players love interacting with NPCs, so the more lifelike they are, the more invested your players will be.

I learned quickly that if I had any NPCs anywhere in my campaign (even if they had nothing to do with the story) I had to give them a name. "I walk into the inn and look around. Is it empty?" If I said it wasn't, my players would always make a point of talking to everyone in the room... and they wanted names for everyone. Be ready for this.

If you need help visualizing locations, consider sketching some maps in the Map section. They don't need to be works of art, just rough outlines to ground yourself as you describe local settings for your players.

Remember, this section is about providing engaging details and story hooks, not huge info dumps. Spread out vivid details over 2-3 pages so players can gradually immerse themselves in the world as they would living in it. With rich, vibrant local settings, your players will be eager to explore your world.

Campaign Summary

Once you've got those pages filled in you can go back to the **Campaign Summary.** The campaign summary is your handy reference guide, condensing the key details of your campaign onto a single page. This cheat sheet will help you keep everything straight when you're in the middle of a game session and need to quickly reference vital information.

Start your campaign summary by writing out a brief overview of the campaign premise. Is it a sprawling epic or a constrained storyline? High fantasy or gritty realism? Tailor the summary to match the genre and scope of the game you have in mind.

Next, jot down the key locations that will feature prominently in the campaign. These could be cities, dungeons, forests, or whatever places are integral to your story. For each location, note any major NPCs, important sites, or other details worth highlighting.

You'll also want to list out the major NPCs in the campaign. Note their name, race, class, location, and a brief description or backstory. Pay special attention to noting any major allies or adversaries.

Speaking of adversaries, your campaign summary should mention any significant villainous groups, dangerous monsters, or other threats the party may face. Even if you plan to keep the primary antagonist mysterious, call out the general danger they represent.

Don't forget to include relevant page number references to any sourcebooks you plan to use. List out the books and page numbers that contain key NPC statistics, location maps, monster details, magical items, etc. This will save you time flipping through books mid-session.

If your campaign relies on custom content beyond the published sourcebooks, make note of that too. List any homebrewed NPCs, locations, magic items, or house rules that the players will encounter.

Finally, leave some blank space to add notes as the campaign unfolds. Scribble down story recaps, new NPCs, or other important developments so you always have the latest info handy.

Keeping your campaign summary nearby makes prep faster and games smoother. With all the key details in one place, you can focus on bringing the story to life, not just looking up facts. Refer back to the summary page frequently and update it each session to track the evolving narrative. By putting in the work upfront to create a robust summary, you'll be equipped to handle anything your players throw at you!

I knew a DM who created a campaign using information from several different d20 compatible games. It really kept the players on their toes! If you plan on doing this, I recommend a handout to each player with rules for leveling up their character in your campaign. Make sure you have it spelled out so there's no confusion.

NPC and Adversary Pages

Now let's head over to the **NPC** and **Adversary** pages. Creating compelling non-player characters (NPCs) and adversaries is one of the most important parts of building your own campaign. These characters will populate your world and interact with your players.

When designing NPCs, start by thinking about their role in the story. Are they a quest giver? A rival faction leader? The blacksmith in a small village? An informant? Determine how they fit into the overall narrative and what purpose they serve.

Next, think about personality and background. Give each NPC distinct traits, ideals, bonds, and flaws using the guides in the Player's Handbook. Come up with a backstory - where are they from? What life events shaped them? How did they get where they are now? Even a simple background brings an NPC to life.

For key NPCs, also consider:

- Appearance - Age, gender, height, build, hair, distinguishing features
- Mannerisms - Do they have any quirks or habits? How do they carry themselves?
- Voice - What do they sound like when they talk? Do they have an accent?
- Secrets - What might the PCs learn about them over time? Hidden agendas or ulterior motives can make NPCs more complex.

Whereas adversaries are actively antagonistic towards the party, NPCs (non-player characters) cover the full range of neutral and allied characters the party will meet. For important NPCs, you'll want to note:

- Name, physical description, and personality - What does the NPC look like and how do they behave?
- Occupation and background - What is the NPC's place in the world? Where are they from originally?
- Location and availability - Where can the party reliably find this NPC? When will they be around?
- Knowledge and capabilities - What information or skills does the NPC have that may assist the party?
- Relationships - Is the NPC connected to other characters and factions the party has interacted with?
- Attitude towards the party - How does the NPC feel about assisting the players? Are they loyal, indifferent, or dubious?
- Dialogue notes - Pre-script or outline any essential dialogue from the NPC to maintain consistency.

For instance, you might create an NPC profile for Lirael Evenstar, an elven ranger willing to guide the party through the Misty Forest for the right price. Her profile would cover her appearance, stern but reliable personality, skill with a longbow, connections to the Elf Queen, neutral attitude towards the party, and a few canned lines of dialogue.

Keeping organized NPC profiles makes playing and improvising hundreds of different characters much more manageable. Leave room to add journal-style notes on how the party's actions shift an NPC's attitudes and availability over time.

When it comes to adversaries, start by deciding if they will be custom-made or pulled from existing sources. If creating your own:

- Give them stats, hit points, armor class, etc using guides in the Dungeon Master's Guide
- Develop combat tactics - How do they fight? Any special attacks or actions?
- Consider lair and minions - Where do they live? Who or what serves them?

- Give them magical abilities, lair actions, and legendary actions as needed to provide an appropriate challenge
- Describe their motivations - What evil plan are they pursuing? Why are they antagonistic to the PCs?

For important adversaries, also give them a backstory and personality beyond just being villainous monsters. Multi-dimensional antagonists create more engaging adventures.

For each adversary, you'll want to note down the following details:

- Name and physical description - What does the adversary look like? Do they have any distinctive features or gear?
- Backstory and motivations - What are this adversary's origins? Why are they antagonistic towards the party? What are their short and long-term goals?
- Abilities and powers - List out the adversary's key combat stats, spells, special traits, etc. How will they try to defeat the party in battle?
- Locations and bases - Where does this adversary operate from? Do they have a lair, base, layer, etc? Are there certain places the party is likely to encounter them?
- Relationships - Does the adversary have allies, minions, rivals, or other connections? Make notes on these relationships.
- Defeat conditions - What will it take for the party to fully defeat or neutralize this adversary? Killing them, destroying an object, fulfilling a prophecy, etc.

For example, you might create an adversary profile for Thazdak the Lich Lord, an undead sorcerer seeking to plunge the world into eternal night. His profile would list his rotting physical appearance, tragic backstory, array of necromantic powers, underground crypt lair, vampire and zombie minions, and the requirement that his phylactery be destroyed to defeat him for good.

Detailed adversary profiles like this help you roleplay recurring villains consistently and make climactic encounters more meaningful. Leave room under each profile to record notes on how the party interacts with and impacts the adversary over time.

Whether crafting intricate quest givers or hordes of nameless goons, well-designed NPCs and adversaries breathe life into your world. Use the guides and prompts in this book to populate your campaign with fun, memorable characters for your players to interact with session after session.

Adversary and NPC Lists

There's an **Adversary List** and an **NPC List** for reference. Use this to keep track of all the adversaries and NPCs your party will (or has) encountered. Use the notes column on the page to keep track of what sourcebook they're in (if any). Keep track of details like locations and interactions. Maintaining thorough, up-to-date adversary and NPC lists takes preparation work upfront, but pays off hugely in terms of game consistency, depth, and storytelling.

With some diligence, the adversary list and NPC list will become invaluable references that help bring your campaign world to life. Refer back to profiles to improvise dialogue and mannerisms consistently, and track how the party's choices change the trajectories of recurring characters over time.

For example: you may want to remember that you have six goblins waiting in the basement of that old farmhouse and one of them wanders up and down the stairs. Or you may want to remember that one of your players talked to that guy at the inn and you named him John and make a note of what they talked about.

Mysteries and Scenarios

There are a few pages for **Mysteries** and **Scenarios**. Think of these as questlines to get your party moving through your adventure. Mysteries and scenarios are key components for creating an engaging campaign. Let's look at each one in more detail.

Mysteries

Mysteries present puzzles and challenges for the party to solve. They create a sense of intrigue and give the players motivation to explore the world. When crafting a mystery:

- Decide on the core question or puzzle at the heart of the mystery. This should be compelling and make the players curious. For example, why did the king's advisor suddenly disappear?
- Create clues that point towards the solution. Spread these out across locations and NPCs. Give the party several ways to uncover each clue.
- Have some "red herring" clues that seem connected but ultimately lead nowhere. This adds realism and complexity.
- Think about how the mystery might unfold depending on the party's actions. Be adaptable if they solve it quicker or miss clues.
- Mysteries can introduce key NPCs, reveal backstory, or set up future scenarios.
- Resist the urge to lead the party step-by-step. Allow them agency in investigating based on the clues they find.

Scenarios

Scenarios (or adventures) provide focused, self-contained stories for one or more game sessions. When planning scenarios:

- Decide on a central conflict, threat, or objective to drive the narrative. Save the world, escape the dungeon, find the artifact etc.
- Sketch out the main NPCs, locations, and encounters connected to the scenario. Flesh these out as needed.
- Create hooks and motivations to pull the party into the scenario. Tie to PC backstories or ongoing plots when possible.
- Decide if the scenario will be more open-ended or railroad-style. Railroading can work for short adventures but don't overdo it.
- Build in flexibility - allow for multiple paths or solutions. Expect the unexpected from players.
- Sketches side plots, red herrings, optional encounters to bring the world alive. Improvise additional details during play.
- Decide on a resolution - climax, finale, reward etc. But be open to alternative endings based on player actions.
- Connect the scenario into the broader campaign. Drop hints, introduce NPCs, reveal lore to seed future adventures.

Remember, every session will not follow a pre-planned scenario. After major adventures, have open-ended sessions focused on PC goals and exploring the world. Scenarios are tools to advance the story, not a straitjacket. Use them judiciously!

The most important thing here to remember is that the players will not follow the path you have in mind. Always create at least three ways to solve a problem... and then watch as they come up with something completely different. I knew a DM who was going to start his campaign with all the players in a cage. He wanted them to fight the guards to escape and was surprised when the rogue picked the lock and the bard charmed the guards into helping them leave.

Don't lead your players or railroad them. I was trying to help a new DM who decided that the easiest way to get the players to do what he wanted was to have an NPC go around with them and lead the group. At one point the NPC was handing out bombs to players and telling them to go and place them in specific areas. The players had no idea why this was happening! There was a "revolt" and they decided the NPC was actually a spy, so they killed him in his sleep.

Loot

Ah yes, loot. What adventuring party doesn't love finding treasure and items after a hard-fought battle? As the Game Master, planning out the loot rewards for your players is an important part of creating a fulfilling campaign. Here are some tips on handling loot in your custom campaign:

Think About Item Rarity

Not every item the party finds needs to be magical and amazing. In fact, mixing in some junk items helps make the truly powerful items feel more special. Come up with a rough idea of how rare you want certain item types to be. For example:

- Mundane items: Common
- Minor magical items: Uncommon
- Major magical items: Rare
- Legendary artifacts: Very rare

Spread out when the party finds rare/legendary items to make them more impactful. Too many too fast makes them feel less special.

Re-skin Existing Items

Don't feel like you have to invent brand new item types from scratch. Take existing items from the core rules and reskin them with a fresh coat of paint. Maybe that Flametongue sword becomes a Frostbrand sword in your icy northern campaign. This saves you work while still making items feel unique.

Make Items Tie Back to the World

Loot feels more meaningful if it connects back to your world and campaign. Maybe they find a dagger used by cultists of the villain, or armor worn by a faction the players are affiliated with. This loot provides insight into the setting.

Consider Consumables Too

Don't forget about potions, scrolls, and other consumable items. These provide one-use powers that can come in handy in a pinch. Tailor the consumables to the types of threats the party will face. Potions of fire resistance for the desert campaign, etc.

Let Players Craft Items

If you have crafting skills in your game, let players use them! Set DCs for different item rarities and have them go on quests to gather ingredients and materials to craft gear. This investment makes the loot more personal.

Provide Item Sets

You can spice up loot progression by having "set items" the party can collect over time. For example, gathering all three pieces of the Pyromancer's Ensemble when combined provides added fire damage and resistance. Set chasing is a great motivation.

Make Loot Personal

The best loot is personalized to a character. Make sure to include items tailored to each PC's build, class, backstory, or interests. This shows you care about them as more than just a pile of combat stats.

That covers the main things to think about when it comes to handing out tantalizing treasures, magical items, and artifacts of wonder! With a bit of creativity and patience, your campaign's loot will feel hand-crafted and special for your players. Just be wary of giving too much too fast, or you might throw off game balance. Use your best judgement and keep the rarity guidelines in mind. Most importantly, have fun dreaming up awesome swag!

I once made a "Sword of Rust" that my players found when rummaging through an abandoned blacksmith's building. It was a +2 to hit, but there was a 50/50 chance they would get tetanus from using it.

Almost all players want to loot *something* during a campaign. Make sure you have this portion figured out or you'll be scrambling to decide what on earth they can loot from a dead wolf.

Random Events/Encounters

Random events and encounters are a great way to add variety, surprise, and fun to your campaign. They break up the monotony of planned story beats and give your players opportunities to think on their feet. This chapter will provide tips on creating engaging random events and encounters that will bring your world to life.

Why Use Random Events and Encounters?

Random events and encounters serve several purposes in a campaign:

- They make the world feel alive and reactive to the players' actions. A world that only exists when the players are present feels flat. Having things happen in the background makes it feel more real.
- They provide moments of surprise and excitement separate from main story beats. Not everything needs to tie into the overarching plot. Fun side adventures keep players engaged.
- They allow you to showcase the environment and cultures of your world. Encounters are opportunities to reveal more about your world.
- They give players additional ways to gain experience, items, allies, enemies, etc. Random events can lead to meaningful gains for players.
- They provide breaks between major story moments. Players need time to digest information before jumping back into tense situations.
- They force players to think on their feet and problem solve. Random situations require creative solutions.

With those benefits in mind, let's look at how to create effective random events and encounters.

Where to Add Random Events and Encounters

Random events and encounters can be added almost anywhere in your campaign, but below are some typical spots:

- While traveling long distances through wilderness, forests, etc. Break up overland travel with interesting distractions.
- When players are residing in a town or city. Bring the streets to life with citizens going about their days.
- While exploring dungeons between planned rooms and monsters. Add some complexity within dungeon corridors.
- During downtime when players are resting or planning. Keep them on their toes during quiet moments.
- Following major story moments as a transition back to normal gameplay. Help players decompress after tense situations.

Get Creative with Events and Encounters

Anything goes when coming up with ideas for random events and encounters! They don't have to tie directly into the main campaign plot. Let your imagination run wild. Here are some examples to inspire you:

- Unusual weather like sudden rainstorms, thick fog, or even a tornado passing nearby. Weather can quickly change the dynamics of travel and combat.
- Natural hazards like forest fires, rockslides, swollen rivers, or crumbling cliffs. These can present danger or block paths, requiring problem solving.
- Wandering merchants with rare items and news from other regions. Players love shopping opportunities.
- Religious processions either joyous or somber. Reveal cultural practices of your world's inhabitants.
- Celebrations and festivals for any number of reasons. These are great chances for players to let loose and have fun.

- A circus caravan providing entertainment and games. Give your players mini-games to participate in.
- Supernatural occurrences like falling stars, auroras, or unexplained sounds. These add mystery and wonder.
- Ruins and abandoned sites to explore with unknown histories. Give players dungeons without context to piece together.
- Wandering enemies like bandits, monsters, or hostile factions. Keep players on guard with potential combat.
- Friendly encounters with allies, guides, refugees, etc. Not everything needs to be a threat.
- Talking animals, plants, fountains, etc. Your world can be as zany as you want it to be!
- Mundane activities like pruning trees, fixing fences, or moving wagons. Not every encounter needs major significance.

Customize Encounters to Your Campaign

When creating random events and encounters, tailor them to fit your campaign's unique world and themes. Ask yourself:

- What environments and terrain would players encounter? Deserts? Seas? Jungles?
- What types of people and settlements exist? Nomads? Farmers? Large cities?
- What cultural practices and history shape the inhabitants? Are there wars, rituals, celebrations?
- What laws and social norms need to be followed? How do guards and laws differ between regions?
- What legends and rumors are passed between people? What superstitions affect them?
- What gods, religions, and magics influence daily life? How does this manifest?
- What flora and fauna exist in your world? Which are unique to certain areas?

29

- What secret societies, fringe groups, and enemies operate out of sight? What signs of their activities appear?
- What lost civilizations or ruins dot the lands? What relics and clues are found?
- How do politics, factions, wars, and power struggles play out? How does news of them spread?
- What mysteries, prophecies, "chosen one" tropes, and fateful stars affect people's thinking?

Brainstorm lists of specific random events and encounters that fit your world. Reuse and remix them as needed during play sessions. Get to know your world intimately.

In one of my first campaigns the players just wanted to go around killing everything that they encountered and looting it. This was tiring as every encounter became a fight. So, I created *the chicken room* in an underground cavern beneath a broken down farmhouse. I'll explain:

The players had been exploring a cavern (all plotlines were pointless by now) and looking for loot. There was a lone chicken sitting atop a chest. The chicken wasn't aggressive, it was just sitting there. The cleric said they were hungry, and the rogue said they were going to open the chest... so they killed the chicken. Just before the rogue could open the chest, two rather aggressive chickens spawned from the dead body. The party quickly killed them... and that's when things got crazy.

Every time they killed a chicken, two sprang up from the dead body. Things got out of hand, and the chickens began piling up in a corner... the weight of all the chickens was killing the ones that sprang up, making more chickens. One chicken doesn't do much damage... but 100 chickens sure do! After 20 minutes they finally stopped trying to kill the chickens and began trying to work together to get out of the cavern.

It was a pivotal moment for the group. They survived the ordeal, but any time they got out of line and reverted back to their 'murder hobo' tendencies I put a chicken or two in the area.

In summary, random events and encounters are tools to make your world feel alive, surprise your players, and reveal more about the environments and cultures you've created. Use them liberally but with purpose. Customize them to reinforce your campaign's unique themes and charm. Keep them varied so players never know what to expect next. With the tips provided, you're ready to bring your world to life with engaging random happenings!

Traps & Puzzles

Adding traps and puzzles to your campaign can provide moments of delight, suspense, and challenge for your players. Used judiciously, they break up combat encounters and force players to think creatively. Overused, they can bring the action to a grinding halt and frustrate players. Follow these tips to incorporate traps and puzzles that enhance your campaign.

Where to Use Traps and Puzzles

- Dungeons - What dungeon would be complete without traps and puzzles? Scatter them throughout, but especially near treasures and in front of the big bad boss lair.
- Wilderness - Traps can make travel interesting, like a covered pit trap on a forest path. Puzzles may be part of larger ruins.
- Urban Environments - Trapped treasure chests, puzzle locks, and "tests" required to gain access to exclusive groups or locations work in cities.
- Everywhere - With creativity, you can justify trapped objects and puzzling situations almost anywhere. Just make sure it fits the environment.

Traps

Traps typically involve dice rolls to detect and disable them. Some common traps include:

- Pit traps - Holes covered with a thin layer of debris to conceal them. Dex saves to avoid falling in.
- Scything blade traps - Blades sweep across a passageway. Dex saves to avoid damage.
- Poison dart traps - Darts shoot from walls when triggered. Dex saves to avoid poison.
- Falling block traps - Stone blocks fall from ceilings. Dex saves to avoid being crushed.

- Fire traps - Flames shoot from holes in walls. Dex saves to avoid damage.
- Spear traps - Spears thrust from walls. Dex saves to avoid being impaled.

When placing traps:

- Foreshadow danger - Describe questionable floor tiles, signs of wear, skulls on spears.
- Allow detection - Let rogues use Thieves' Tools to detect and disarm traps.
- Give clues - After failure, hint at the trap's nature so they can avoid it.
- Limit dead ends - Avoid unavoidable instant-kill traps.

Puzzles

Puzzles rely on the players' reasoning, not their characters' abilities. Types include:

- Riddles - Rhyming or word puzzle questions. Answer to open doors, disarm traps.
- Pattern recognition - Find the patterns in sequences of images, colors, sounds. Replicate to open passages.
- Physical puzzles - Manipulate components like sliding tiles to form images, connect pipes, or decode a lock.
- Logic puzzles - Discern the rules governing a magic square, maze, or mystical object. Manipulate according to those rules.
- Cryptograms - Decode scrambled alphabets on inscriptions to reveal secret messages.
- Ciphers - Translate numeric codes based on provided key.

When designing puzzles:

- Match difficulty to party - If too hard, it's frustrating. If too easy, it's boring.

- Provide clues - Incrementally reveal details to help them along.
- Consider multiple solutions - Don't get wedded to only one way to solve it.
- Have a backup plan - In case they can't figure it out, provide an alternative route.
- Make optional - Important areas shouldn't hinge solely on solving a puzzle.

With clever use of traps and puzzles, you can challenge your players, force creative problem solving, and add an element of fun to your campaign! Just use them in moderation and stay flexible if they get stuck. With practice, you'll master the art of traps and puzzles your players will love.

Example number 1: I played in a campaign where the DM had such an elaborate puzzle that none of us could figure it out. To this day (several years after the campaign ended) none of us know what the answer to the puzzle was. Heck, I don't even remember the puzzle!

Example number 2: I had two booby-trapped bridges across a chasm. The rogue kept failing at her attempts to check for traps. After three failed attempts (she wasn't able to roll higher than a 6) the barbarian decided the bridge was okay and started to run across one of them. He fell 30 feet. The party got down there, healed him, and then *went back up to where they were*. Cue bridge number two and the same results.

Player Characters and Back Stories

The Player Character section is one of the most important parts of creating your own campaign. This is where you will gather key information about the heroes of your story - the player characters. It's a good idea to copy these details straight off the players' character sheets.

Once you have the basics down for each character, consider adding a portrait or visual reference. This will help you and your players visualize each hero. Feel free to get creative - drawings, magazine clippings, or printed photos all work.

You may also want to include a brief backstory written by each player. One or two paragraphs explaining where their character came from and what led them to this point in their adventuring career.

Backstories are useful for giving PCs added depth and connections to your world. However, keep them reasonably broad so they don't limit your options as GM later on. You can always expand on backstories through gameplay.

In addition to individual backstories, think about relationship dynamics between party members. Are some PCs old friends or rivals? Do they share any connections through past adventures? Leaving some ties undefined allows opportunities to develop bonds organically in early gameplay.

Once your player character section is filled out, you'll have a strong sense of who your protagonists are. Refer back frequently when planning adventures to ensure each hero has a chance to shine based on their traits and backstories. Get to know them well - these PCs are the heart of your campaign!

Back Stories

Backstories are a great way to give your player characters added history and personality. They connect your PCs to your homebrew world, giving them a stake in the unfolding events.

As Game Master, work with each player individually to craft backstories. The players know their characters best, so let them take the lead on key relationships and formative events. However, you have final say to veto anything that doesn't fit your campaign.

Aim for backstories that are 1-2 paragraphs long. They should paint a vivid picture of the PC's origins but leave plenty of room for you to fill in details. Avoid overly complex or limiting storylines.

Good backstories tie into your world and campaign themes. They provide built-in story hooks and connections you can incorporate throughout your adventures.

Here are some examples of backstory elements that lend themselves well to ongoing campaign play:

- Important NPC connections such as family members, mentors, rivals, etc. These relationships give you NPCs to involve.
- Unresolved mysteries from the PC's past like unknown parentage, disappeared mentors, unavenged losses, etc. You can build adventures around investigating these mysteries.
- Wrongs to be righted or scores to settle provide motivations that drive a PC's goals. These often lead to encounters as they pursue vengeance or justice.
- Keepsakes, heirlooms, or treasures that connect to the PC's history. You can use these unique items in your campaign when appropriate.
- Secrets known only to the PC and GM. These can lead to great roleplaying moments if handled well. Slowly reveal related clues but save the big reveal for the right moment.

The key is balance - enough detail to feel real, but not so much that you're locked into specifics. Leave room to adjust backstories to fit emerging events in your ongoing campaign story.

Backstories are a collaborative effort between player and GM. Talk through ideas and find connections that excite you both. This extra care makes for richer PCs that feel like real parts of your world.

I played in a campaign where the DM and I worked together with my back story. My character had a major secret that only the two of us knew. Anyone finding out my secret too soon in the campaign would have ended the campaign... we all would die! There were several times I thought the party was going to find out my secret before the DM was ready.

Notes and Maps

As you reach the finale of crafting your campaign, don't forget the importance of taking thorough notes during gameplay. As Game Master, comprehensive notes will be invaluable for keeping track of the unfolding story, NPCs met, clues uncovered, and locations visited.

Purchase my **Game Master's Companion** and use it as your official campaign journal. Record session summaries, including major events, conversations, and decisions. Jot down NPC names, motivations, secrets, and other details. Note clues, mysteries, and plot threads as they emerge and develop. List notable locations, factoids, and lore.

Your **Game Master's Companion** helps you maintain continuity and refer back to past occurrences. If a player asks "Didn't we meet a sailor named Tom at that port city a few sessions ago?" you can consult your notes for the answer. Detailed notes also aid you in foreshadowing future events and plotting how storylines will advance.

Leave space to record session statistics like XP awarded, magic items found, etc. Having this data on hand lets you ensure game balance and gives you insight into what rewards make sense for your group.

In addition to the **Game Master's Companion**, organize any handouts, printouts, or other physical materials into a folder or binder. Keep maps, letters from NPCs, cursed tomes, and other handouts together for easy reference.

Maps bring your world to life in a tactile way while giving players critical environmental context during gameplay. Decide if you want to use "theater of the mind" abstract descriptions or physical maps with miniature tokens.

For theater of the mind games, vividly describe locations, distances, borders, and other geographic details to set the scene.

Occasionally sketch simple maps to give players a general sense of important locations.

If using full maps and miniatures, decide on your scale (1 inch = 5 feet is common). Craft maps for important story locations, complete with terrain like walls, water, and difficult ground. Make "DM versions" with secret doors and Passages, and "player versions" without.

Maps can be hand-drawn, printed from programs, or created using 3D terrain. Fill your maps with evocative sites like tombs, castles, caverns, and ruins. Leave room for players to venture to uncharted territories.

Carefully consider how much of your world you wish to map out in advance. Some DMs map entire continents before starting. Others reveal the world session by session. Do what fits your personal style.

Most importantly let your maps inspire epic adventures! With cartography guiding their journey, your players will have memorable escapades across the lands you chart for them. Onward to adventures beyond the edges of the map!

As a general rule, I like to tell future game masters to remember that you created the world and the "problems" but it's the players who live in it, drive it, fix it and change it.

Have fun and may all your rolls be Nat 20s!

Appendix: Images From Chronicles of Adventure: The Ultimate RPG Campaign Builder

Adversaries Image

Adversary Name:
Appearance:

Catch Phrase:

Background:

Key Information: goals, special moves, etc
1
2
3

Roleplaying Cues: mannerisms, physical actions, accent, etc
1
2
3

Stat Block

Adversary List Image

Adversary List		
Type	Location	Notes

Page 47

Back Stories Image

Back Stories		
Player/Character:		

Page 19

43

Brainstorming Image

Brainstorming
Idea:
Problem or Goal:
Setting or Location:
Important Characters:
Adventure Hook:
Midpoint Surprise:
Cool Climax:
Problem or Goal:
Clues or Secrets:
To Do List:

Campaign Summary Image

Campaign Summary

Campaign Title

Outline

System

Plotlines	Goals

Important Locations	Main NPC's/Allies

Main Adversaries

Books Used	Page Numbers

Local Settings Image

Local Settings: broad content

Loot Image

Loot			
Item	Description	Stats	Value

Mysteries Image

Mysteries	
Goal	
Clue 1	
Clue 2	
Clue 3	
Details	

Page 32

48

Notes Image

Notes

NPC List Image

NPC List		
Type/Name	Location	Notes

Page 59

50

NPCs Image

NPC Name:
Appearance:
Catch Phrase:
Background:

Key Information: essential interaction or information that the players are supposed to get from the NPC

1
2
3

Roleplaying Cues: mannerisms, physical actions, accent, etc

1
2
3

Stat Block

What Do My Players Need to Know for Character Creation Image

What Do My Players Need to Know for Character Creation

Player Characters Image

Player Characters

Character:	Player:

Race:	Class:	Multiclass:
Level:	Darkvision/Low Light:	Languages:

Appearance Notes:

Backstory Submitted? Yes No | Backstory Added: Yes No | Completed? Yes No

Subplots/Secrets:

Character:	Player:

Race:	Class:	Multiclass:
Level:	Darkvision/Low Light:	Languages:

Appearance Notes:

Backstory Submitted? Yes No | Backstory Added: Yes No | Completed? Yes No

Subplots/Secrets:

Character:	Player:

Race:	Class:	Multiclass:
Level:	Darkvision/Low Light:	Languages:

Appearance Notes:

Backstory Submitted? Yes No | Backstory Added: Yes No | Completed? Yes No

Subplots/Secrets:

Character:	Player:

Race:	Class:	Multiclass:
Level:	Darkvision/Low Light:	Languages:

Appearance Notes:

Backstory Submitted? Yes No | Backstory Added: Yes No | Completed? Yes No

Subplots/Secrets:

Character:	Player:

Race:	Class:	Multiclass:
Level:	Darkvision/Low Light:	Languages:

Appearance Notes:

Backstory Submitted? Yes No | Backstory Added: Yes No | Completed? Yes No

Subplots/Secrets:

Random Events/Encounters Image

Random Events/Encounters
Occurrence Chances:
Die Rolls:
Encounter Details:
Wandering Encounters:
Periodic Events:
Rewards

Page 37

Scenarios Image

Scenarios
Hook
Timeline
Triggers
Rewards
Details

Page 33

55

The World Image

The World: high level summary

Traps/Puzzles Image

Traps/Puzzles
Description:
Misdirection/Guise:
Mechanics or Effects:
What Won't Work:
How to Avoid/Circumvent:
Disarming Attempts:
Guards/Wards/Triggers:
Motives:
Clue 1:
Clue 2:
Clue 3:
Solution 1:
Solution 2:
Solution 3:
Rewards:

Epilogue

And so the chronicle comes to an end, the saga of adventure that began with Chronicles of Adventure: The Ultimate RPG Campaign Builder has culminated in this guide to crafting your own epic tales. Through the twists and turns of building worlds, populating them with compelling characters, and sending your players on missions of danger and discovery, you now have all the tools needed to weave an unforgettable story.

Yet, as every game master knows, no plan survives contact with the players. They will inevitably go off script, come up with wild schemes, and send your carefully plotted campaign careening in unexpected directions. So, while this tome provides everything needed to build the foundations of adventure, the wise GM must also prepare for the chaos that players will unleash.

That is why the next volume in this series will be Chronicles of Adventure: The Ultimate RPG Game Master's Book of Chaos. Within its pages you'll find advice on improvisation when your players go off the rails, tools for generating unexpected twists and surprises, and guidance for running a fluid, flexible story that can adapt to your players' antics. Be prepared for when your adventures descend into glorious chaos! The Game Master's Book of Chaos will give you the tools you need to think on your feet and respond with agility when plans collapse and pandemonium reigns.

Stay tuned for the next thrilling installment of the Chronicles of Adventure! Your journeys into the world of game mastering have only just begun....

Other Books by Amy N Kaplan

Free Range Pigs: An Interactive Adventure Story About Three Little Pigs

Free Range Bears: An Interactive Adventure Story About Three Bears

Free Range Goats: An Interactive Adventure Story About Ten Little Goats

Nigel Needs A Home

Chronicles of Adventure: The Ultimate RPG Player's Companion

Chronicles of Adventure: The Ultimate RPG Game Master's Companion

Chronicles of Adventure: The Ultimate RPG Campaign Builder

Becoming Jewish – A Journey to Spiritual Freedom

With Ink-Stained Fingers and a Heart Brimming with Stories – Words

Free Range RPG Player Journal

Free Range RPG GM Journal

Free Range RPG Campaign Builder

Watch For These Exciting New Titles

Free Range Wolves: An Interactive Adventure Story about Three Wolves

Chronicles of Adventure: The Ultimate RPG Game Master's Book of Chaos Volume 1

Chronicles of Adventure: The Ultimate RPG Game Master's Book of Chaos Volume 2

Whispers of the Heart

Carnival of Shadows

The Stone From the Dreamtime

About the Author

Amy N. Kaplan is an experienced game master devoted to helping others craft epic tabletop adventures. As the author of the bestselling Chronicles of Adventure series, she provides roleplayers with indispensable tools to build immersive worlds, vivid characters, and thrilling quests. Amy brings decades of expertise honed while running her own game store. When she isn't writing RPG supplements, you can find her rolling dice with her family or discussing her favorite fandoms. Amy's passion empowers gamers to unlock their greatest storytelling potential.

http://www.amynkaplan.com

Milton Keynes UK
Ingram Content Group UK Ltd.
UKHW040757180324
439696UK00001B/33

9 781962 613064